Unblocked
The sure-fire way to get rid of writer's block forever

Caroline Frechette

UNBLOCKED ©2015 by Caroline Frechette. All rights reserved. No part of this book may be used or reproduced in any manner whatsoever without written permission except in the case of brief quotations in critical articles and reviews. For more information, contact Renaissance Press. First edition.
Cover art and design by Caroline Frechette. Interior design and graphics by Caroline Frechette. Edited by L.P. Vallee and Evelyn Cimesa.
Legal deposit, Library and Archives Canada, October 2015.
Paperback 978-1-987963-04-5
Ebook ISBN 978-1-987963-05-2
Renaissance Press
http://renaissancebookpress.com
info@renaissancebookpress.com

Unblocked
The sure-fire way to get rid of writer's block forever

Introduction

Not a week goes by without me seeing a social media post from a writer asking for help with their writer's block. That question is invariably met with writing prompt websites or other methods for generating ideas. That isn't bad advice in and of itself; sometimes the problem really is that you would like to write a story, but don't know where to start.

However, I have found that most writers who ask for advice aren't lacking ideas. The majority of them have an idea they are developing, but are stuck at some stage and unable to move forward. Or, in some cases, they have too many ideas, and get stuck trying to decide which is best. In all those cases, more ideas just won't help: they are likely to get stuck in the same place again.

Writer's block isn't a simple problem, and there isn't a single, fix-everything solution. That isn't to say that there isn't a solution at all, but just as you can't possibly go see your doctor and tell them "I'm sick" and be given a medication that will cure anything you could have, you can't just say "I have writer's block" and expect to find one single solution. Just as with illnesses, the process of diagnosis is essential to finding the right solution to the problem.

This books will allow you to self-diagnose your writer's block, and will provide a list of possible solutions to specific problems. I hope it helps you banish the obstacles which are holding you back right now, and that it serves again and again when that block manifests itself in any and all of its forms.

Table of Contents

Introduction

  Do you have writer's block?   1

    So what causes us to get stuck?   2

Part 1 Causes related to content   3

  Chapter 1: Staring at a blank page   5

    Reading   6

    People-watching   6

    Extrapolation   7

    Writing exercises   8

    Brainstorming   10

  Chapter 2: You know what you want to write about, but you still can't start   13

  Chapter 3: Those pesky characters have thrown a wrench in the works   15

  Chapter 4: The story has a mind of its own   17

  Chapter 5: A piece of the puzzle is missing   23

  Chapter 6: The end is coming... too soon   27

  Chapter 7: You just can't write that next scene   31

  Chapter 8: You need more information   33

Part 2: Causes related to Form · 37

- Chapter 9: Narrative voice problems · 39
- Chapter 10: Point of view problems · 41
- Chapter 11: Pacing problems · 45
- Chapter 12: Tone problems · 47
- Chapter 13: Description problems · 49

Part 3: Personal Causes · 51

- Chapter 14: Loss of enthusiasm about the story · 53
- Chapter 15: Too many new ideas · 55
- Chapter 16: The wrong environment · 59
- Chapter 17: Taking care of your body · 63
- Chapter 18: Knowing your natural cycle · 65
- Chapter 19: What will my mother think? · 69
- Chapter 20: Writing life blues · 73
- Chapter 21: Real life is taking over · 77
- Chapter 22: Poor self-esteem · 79
- Chapter 23: Fear of failure · 83
- Chapter 24 Mental health issues · 87
  - How to make writing truly therapeutic · 90

Acknowledgements · 93
Resources · 95
Character questionnaire · 97
About the author · 103
A word from the author · 105

DO YOU HAVE WRITER'S BLOCK?

Creative blocks are something every artist struggles with, especially writers. When most people think of writer's block, they picture a writer staring at an empty page anxiously. In French, it's even called *syndrome de la page blanche*, or "white page syndrome." For a few people, that is exactly the form it takes: they want to write, but are lacking ideas. Others know that they're blocked, and the fact that they are blocked is on their mind all the time, and they can't think of anything else than the block. But, in most cases, writer's block takes a far more subtle and insidious form: avoidance.

People who suffer from writer's block will often find themselves wanting to do something else as soon as they're supposed to be writing. Suddenly, cleaning out the closet or finally taking down the Christmas decorations becomes a pressing priority, something that can't wait any longer. Other times, it can *feel* like you're doing productive work, for example, surfing the internet looking for fonts, or planning the cover of that book you're not writing, to forget the fact that you keep trying to write the same paragraph, only you hit backspace as much as you type.

So what causes us to get stuck?

The actual causes behind writer's block can be grouped into three categories: content issues, form issues, and, most prevalent and important of all, personal and environmental issues.

The first section of this book starts with the "white page syndrome", or beginning-of-the-story block, with a chapter on how to generate ideas. If, however, you are among the majority who get stuck at a later point in your story, please read on!

Part 1

Causes related to content

Content-related writer's block is probably the easiest to solve. This, along with issues relating to form, has to do with the story itself. And, even though you might feel stuck, the problem isn't your ability to write, but the elements of the specific story you're writing. The solutions to these kinds of problems, while not always obvious to the writer struggling with a block, can be relatively straightforward, if not necessarily simple.

Some content-related issues apply mostly to planners, and others are more common in "pantsers" (people who "write by the seat or their pants", without a plan) so whether you fall into one category or the other, you may find something useful for you here.

Chapter 1

Staring at a Blank Page

Although it's certainly not the most common cause, it does happen that you want to write, but just don't have an idea what about. I will address this here, and move on to the much more common form of writer's block, which usually happens partway through a story. If you are struggling with middle-of-the-book writer's block, please feel free to skip ahead to the next chapter.

There are a lot of different techniques out there to generate and gather ideas. Eventually, some of them will become a second nature, and you'll have more ideas than you know what to do with.

READING

Reading regularly is probably the most important thing you can do as a writer. Being exposed to the written word is how you learn how to write. It helps you see a variety of styles and voices, and gives you a good idea of how it could be done.

But more importantly, and more relevant to the question at hand, reading can be a great source of inspiration. Not in the way you think: I'm not suggesting you read stories to take their content. But a creative mind needs downtime to recharge, and food to grow on. When you read, you give your mind the time it needs to rest, and the food it needs to grow new ideas. Instead of being idle, when exposed to stories, the mind contemplates possibilities while relaxing, and you'll likely get new and fresh ideas just by providing your brain with some restful stimulation. However, if you keep trying to create stories without ever replenishing your mind, you will hit a wall for sure; I've seen it happen over and over again. The most productive students I had, the ones with the most original ideas, were always the avid readers.

PEOPLE-WATCHING

Most experienced writers are skilled observers of the world. Yes, they are often lost in thought and, yes, they are often distracted, but that doesn't mean they don't keenly observe the world and people around them. In fact, it is that sense of observation and wonder that generates the most, and the best, ideas.

Just keeping an eye out for how people behave, how they speak to each other, and how they react to the different situations they are in is essential to a writer. To write good, realistic characters, you have to be very aware of how the human psyche works, what makes people unique, different from each other.

As much as you should observe how people act, you should also wonder about them. Every time you go to a public place, take a moment to observe people, and wonder. What are they thinking about? What are they doing? Where are they going? What did they just do? More often than not, you will find a seed for at least a character, if not a story.

Finally, you should speak to as many people as you can. Speak, and *listen*. Everyone has an experience that is unique to them, and you might see a different side of the world just by spending a few minutes a day speaking to a stranger. Seek out those who are different from you! If people sit next to you on the bus and start talking, engage them! Hear what they have to say. You never know what you'll take away from that encounter.

EXTRAPOLATION

Beyond observing people, you should try and keep up with the news. Look into new scientific discoveries, political changes in the world, wars, laws, etc. When you see great change in the world, wonder what the social implications of these changes are. How could it change the people it affects? What would happen if it was taken one step further?

Nearly all science-fiction is based on this type of idea. What if robots rose up against humans? What if machines decided to use humans as a power source? What if a virus engineered to be a weapon got loose and killed most of humanity?

It might not lead to stories right away, but taking the habit of looking at world events and wondering "What if...?" will definitely plant a few seeds along the way.

If you take up the habits of people-watching and extrapolating on new information, you should never want for ideas. However, you might still need something specific, or a quick way to generate ideas once in a while. In those situations, the following exercises help a great deal.

Writing exercises

Writing prompts

A writing prompt is something which is meant to provoke inspiration. It is a sort of theme, which gives a basic idea for a story. The writer usually looks at the prompt and writes a short fiction (or sometimes longer) from what it inspires. There are two kinds of prompts: written and visual.

Written prompts

Written prompts are usually sentences, sometimes short paragraphs, or even randomly selected words, which are meant to spark inspiration and provoke a story. There are quite a few sources for writing prompts out there. For example, there are multiple phone apps that you can download and install on your phone which do exactly this, a new one every day. All you have to do is search under "writing prompt" in your app store, and you should find a few free ones.

There are also a few websites, which are updated regularly, and offer a wealth of very good prompts. You can find those in the ***Resources*** section of this book.

Another writing prompt technique, which can be quite fun, consists in writing a few words which correspond to the categories of "character", "place" and "object", and to randomly draw one from each category. You then have to write a story which features all three elements.

Visual prompts

To me, visual prompts have always been immensely more stimulating than written ones, and I've found that my students have also produced some of their best work from the visual prompts exercise in my class. Visual prompts usually come in the form of a picture, but they can also come from an object. For pictures, just look at the picture and wonder what the scene represents. What is happening? What was going on before? What will happen right after? I have always found that googling artistic photos (just search for famous photographers, such as Robert Doisneau, Diane Arbus, Annie Leibovitz, Nan Goldin) is a great source of inspiration; they are always pictures taken in the middle of action. Another site that I like a lot for writing inspiration is **http://postsecret.com/**. It's a site where people write and illustrate their deepest secret, without a context, and send them on a postcard. Those secrets can be very powerful story seeds!

Objects can be a great source of prompts too. Going to a thrift store and looking at all the knick-knacks can be incredibly inspiring. Who owned this? How did they come by it? What did they do with it? Why is it here now?

FREEWRITING

Freewriting is an exercise in which you start writing, with or without a prompt, and you don't stop, take a break or put your pen down for a set amount of time, usually five or ten minutes. You write whatever comes to mind, and you have to keep writing, even if that means actually writing "I don't know what to write." This can allow you to get in touch with your subconscious, and find new seeds for ideas or maybe develop ideas which are in very early stages.

Brainstorming

Brainstorming is an exercise which, in its most basic form, consists in throwing together as many ideas in as short a time as possible.

Group brainstorming

Group brainstorming consists in getting a group together to generate ideas on a specific subject, or possible answers to a specific question. To make sure that the maximum potential of this exercise is reached, there must be some rules. For example, no judgement is allowed. People must feel like they can speak freely, and not have their ideas ridiculed, or they will hold back certain things that may seem ridiculous to them but may have been useful. It is also important to say everything which comes to mind, because often the mind cannot move on to the next idea if the previous one hasn't been said. To make sure that everything is recorded and that all parties remain respectful, it is often useful to elect a leader for the process, who will write down the ideas, and will also be in charge of keeping the session on topic.

Solo brainstorming

Solo brainstorming is usually done in the form of cluster brainstorming, or mind-mapping. Basically, the technique consists in writing down one word or idea, then circling it, and writing ideas related to that first idea, circling them, and writing out other ideas related to those ideas, and so on.

You can do this until you generate all the ideas you need to get started in your story.

There is a free site which allows you to do mind-mapping online, exactly as you would on paper: **http://bubbl.us/**

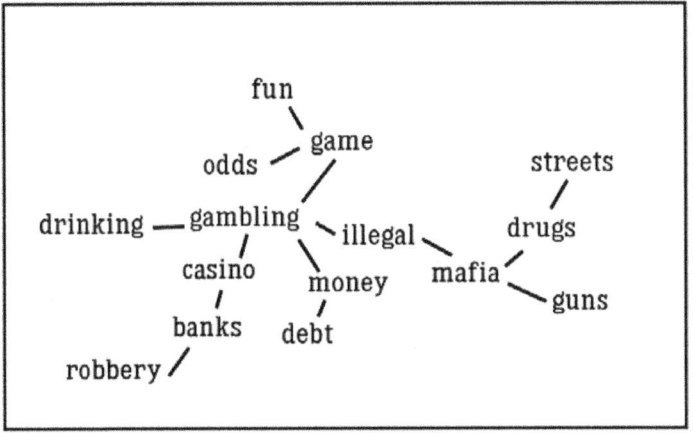

An example of cluster brainstorming. With this simple session done in five minutes and started with the word "game," it's easy to see how someone could find the basis of a very complete crime story.

Chapter 2

You know what you want to write about, but you still can't start

So, you *have* an idea for a story, perhaps even a complete outline. Still, you can't seem to get started on what you want to write, because those first words just won't come out.

This can be due to several reasons. First of all, it might be one of many personal reasons preventing you from starting: panic at writing about something outside of your comfort zone, because you don't think you can do it, because you're not sure you're any good, etc. I go through each and every one of these in part 3 of this book, and I strongly encourage you to take a look at those if you're having a hard time starting.

That being said, there are some content concerns that can keep you from getting started at all. One of the main ones would be not knowing exactly *where* to start, as in which scene, which specific moment in the story to begin with.

The start of a story, the very first line, the moment that you use to introduce your reader to the story, is incredibly important. If done right, it will draw your reader into the story, engage him or her with your characters, and ensure that he or she will keep reading. If done poorly, it might cause your book to go unread. Knowing that, it can become paralyzing to know exactly the right moment to pick when beginning a new story. Even if you know everything that happens afterward, that doesn't mean you know exactly where to start.

There is a simple solution to that problem: just start. Anywhere. It doesn't matter. Yes, I know, of course it *matters* where you start your novel, but at the first draft stage, it really doesn't matter, because when you rewrite and/or revise, you can change where the story starts. You can add a scene if it doesn't start early enough, or, more likely, you can remove extraneous scenes in the beginning, so it doesn't really matter where you start. Give yourself permission to start at a time that isn't exactly perfect for your story; it'll help you move forward. Nothing is set in stone until the book is printed.

Another solution is to start somewhere else than the beginning. Stories don't have to be written in a linear fashion; it's okay to start at another point in the story, later, at a scene you really visualized and are ready to write. Maybe it'll help you get to know your story and characters well enough to go back toward the beginning and pick that perfect scene. However, if you write your story out of order, it's likely you'll have more editing and rewriting work to do before it's ready than if you had started in the wrong place to begin with. Still, it might be what works best for your composition style.

Chapter 3

Those pesky characters have thrown a wrench in the works

This is one of the most common content-related causes for writer's block. If you are someone who likes to discover their characters as the story evolves, chances are this happened to you at least once before: you had a plan for where your characters or story were going, whether it was a firm outline or just a vague idea, and it just can't happen that way anymore. Either your characters have gone off on a completely different path, or they have become people who are not able to do the things you need them to be doing.

This problem, while being a very common one, is unfortunately one that does not have an easy solution. It has a solution, in fact many of them, but they require a lot of work to fix it.

It should be said before you read on that, even though sometimes you do need to change your mind about some things, or make radical changes to your story, it doesn't mean anything has to be deleted forever. Instead of hitting "delete," you should take up the habit of copying and pasting those snippets in a "dump" file. That way, you get to use them later in other stories, or even use them as a sort of bonus material on the release of your novel, like DVD deleted scenes.

The easiest solution is to re-plan the rest of the book with the character changes in mind. Change that event that you need to happen, re-write your outline if need be. I know it's disappointing to have to change your mind, and chances are, you already know that this is what you need to do, but are looking for another solution, and the one which involves the least actual changes to your story.

Another solution would be to rework the beginning, and remove or change the event(s) which changed your character into the person that just isn't likely to do the things you need them to do. This definitely demands that you first deeply understand your character's psyche, and it might mean that you need to rewrite a few of the scenes which reference that event.

The last solution to this problem is to remove the character entirely from the beginning of the story, and replace him with a character who would be able to evolve in the direction you need them to. This is probably the most difficult solution, but sometimes it's what your story needs. This *might* allow you to keep your story events straight, but it's also likely you'll be stuck with the same problem at some other point in your story, as your new character, being different than the original, is likely to not do the exact same things as your original character did, so you might have to change some of the events as well. However, you might discover that this new character takes your story in much more interesting places, and interacts with it and the other characters in a much better way than before.

Chapter 4

The story has a mind of its own

Sometimes, the characters do something, or a certain course of events provokes an idea in you that makes you look at your plan and think "Ooooooh... this is SO much more interesting." And at that moment, it was the best idea ever (and it may very well still be). Only now, a few scenes or chapters later, your story is off course, and you're not sure how to logically bring it back to its original chain of events, or to that scene you had in mind when you started writing the book, or to that ending which makes your story worthwhile.

That one is tough, and the solutions aren't easy to accept. There are really only two things you can do if that is the reason you're stuck. The first one is to redo your plan from that point on, using the post-it method, which I explain below, to try and bring your story back on track.

The second solution is again to re-plan the end of your story, but to discard the scene or ending you had in mind, opting for a new one altogether, which fits your new direction better.

In either of these choices, the post-it method will definitely help you. I call it the "post-it method" because I like to use sticky notes, but you can do so on index cards, or using Scrivener. I consider it the easiest and most efficient way to outline a novel. Its non-linear process helps naturally eliminate surplus or nonessential scenes because you tend to look at them strictly for their function in moving the story forward, and not try to just come up with what comes next in your story, stalling for time or word count when you're not sure where your story is going.

All you need is a pen and a pack of post-its (or masking tape and index card, or sticky tack and cut up pieces of paper... basically something you can stick to a wall and remove and reposition easily, or a software that allows you to do that, even Word with cut and paste works great) and a piece of blank wall somewhere (if you're working with physical materials, which I personally prefer). I have used the staircase, the headboard of my bed, my kitchen cabinets, the closet door... there's always a space in your house that you can use to do this. And don't worry about needing to have it up there for a couple of days or more; this method is so easy you shouldn't be spending more than a few hours outlining an entire novel.

Step 1: timelines

The first thing I want you to do is if you know you're going to have subplots, divide your space into the amount of "timelines" equivalent to these subplots. You can make those into rows or columns (I personally find rows easier to work with, but you may be very tall and have a narrow wall, in which case columns might work better).

Step 2: the best scenes

Next, you should write out your favorite scenes, the ones you had in mind when you came up with that story, on individual post-its. In the particular case of restructuring your novel, you should write out what you have already written in your book, scene by scene, and then do the same thing with the scenes you want to preserve in the rest of your outline. Don't write out the full scene; just one sentence summarizing the main action in that scene.

Step 3: filling in the blanks

Put the scenes you have written up in the timelines where they belong in relative order of causality. Even if you're doing a deconstructed story (for example *Pulp Fiction,* or *Memento*), your outline should be done in order of causality just to make sure you've wrapped up everything; you can deconstruct it later.

After that comes the hardest part (and it's really not that bad). You need to fill the spaces in between your scenes so that the reader has all the information that they need to appreciate and understand those scenes (and obviously, the climax). That can be events, character development, etc. Come up with all the scenes that you need to provide that information, and put them up there, until your main plot and all your subplots are wrapped up nicely and there are no loose ends.

You don't need to come up with those scenes chronologically; just write up the answers as they come to you, and organize them in order of causality until there are no more gaps to fill and all the essential information is up on your board.

Typically, a novel would have around 30-40 post-its (at a rate of one post-it per scene), if you're going for a 50-80k average.

Step 4: putting it all together
That is the easiest part. Basically, take all your timelines, and put them together in one great timeline, deciding which bits of timelines interact with others, creating the natural rhythm of your story. This is also the part where you can deconstruct your timelines, in the case of an anti-structure storyline.

Sometimes, you'll find that two post-its work together as one scene. It might be because one was an event, and one was a bit of character development, and you didn't come up with them at the same time, or you put them in separate plot lines, and now you see they fit together in one scene. Just merge these two story beats by sticking the post-its together.

Step 5: get that stuff off the wall before your child eats it or your roommate throws it away
If I'm lazy, I usually take down the post-it notes and stick them directly in a book, in the order they go in. Then, because I don't want to lose that book, eventually I can transcribe that outline to Word (or whatever software you are using) and *BACK IT UP.*

There's nothing wrong with having to re-draft a story that you feel has veered off course. I've had to do this often enough, for example, in *Blood Relations*, I ended up completely changing my mind about things; two characters who met and were supposed to hate each other instead became instantly fond of each other, and another character that was meant to play a role in the series died in the first book. It was what made sense at the time, and I redrafted my plan accordingly. In *Making a Living,* I found that my chapters were too long, and I had to cut them up; I also found that the two main characters were connected in ways I hadn't foreseen; I had to rewrite a whole lot of the beginning to make it fit. It can be discouraging, but the result is usually very satisfying.

Besides, it's better to have to re-draft a book than to just abandon it altogether. Sometimes, though, it's okay to take a break from your work, put it aside, and write something else until you're ready to face the work that has to be done on your story.

CHAPTER 5

A PIECE OF THE PUZZLE IS MISSING

Contrary to the first two common problems, which are typical in planners, this one happens mostly to people who dive in without a plan; while there is nothing wrong with that method, and in fact it can be really fun to write that way, it can also happen that sometimes, you reach a point where you can't figure out what happens next, and that is why you're blocked.

Generally speaking, this problem happens when you write a story and have an important element of the story that remains to be figured out. If you are in the habit of "pantsing," or writing by the seat of your pants, as it were, chances are you're used to starting with no clear idea of what's ahead, and having those gaps fill themselves by the natural flow of the story. But it does happen sometimes that the gaps *don't* fill themselves out, and you can reach a point where you can't go on.

It can be really interesting, for example, to write a mystery to which you don't know the solution; for one, it can maximize your chances of the reader NOT finding out who the killer is at page ten, but you need to know who did it eventually. And although you can go back when you have the solution and sprinkle the appropriate clues to make sure to have all the elements necessary to make your "big reveal" plausible, it can happen that you reach a point where your detective has to figure out the solution... but you still haven't. Needless to say, you will remain unable to write that next scene until you figure out what the solution to your mystery is. I suggest writing a brief list of what you have so far in terms of clues, and seeing what fits best: you can make that your solution, or even your red herring, if you have another viable option.

This doesn't apply only to mysteries, either. Really, it can be any part of a story. Sometimes, it's character motivation that is missing, and we can reach a point where we actually can't find a good explanation for how this character's been acting, and unfortunately the time has come where you need to explain these motivations that you don't understand. Or, it comes to us what exactly the motivation is, but suddenly some of the things that character has been doing make no sense anymore. If that is the case, there are a few things that you can do to fix this. Obviously if some of the things that your character has been doing now make no sense because of the motivation you've decided upon, then you need to remove those things from your manuscript.

But if you're still having a hard time coming up with your character's motivations, then there are a few character building exercises which might help you. Perhaps it is that you don't know the character well enough to come up with a motivation; in that case, I suggest filling out a character questionnaire. You will find an example of this at the end of this book, in the ***Resources***, and you can also print one off my website **http://carolinefrechette.com/character-questionnaire/**.

Or, maybe you *do* know the character but you're just not sure why he or she is doing some of those things. If that is what's happening, I suggest doing a character interview. The character interview is an exercise in which you sit down with a pen and paper (or a keyboard, if you are so inclined) and actually have a conversation with your character. Ask them questions you would ask if you were conducting a real interview, and you can ask them outright what they want. Depending on their personality, some characters might tell you off at first, but be persistent, eventually they will talk to you. I find this a great way to get to know characters that are extremely different from who I am; I get to ask them what they think directly, and why they behave a certain way, and it makes things a lot clearer.

Another thing that might be missing from your story and have you stuck is exactly how it ends. Often, you can start with a general idea of how the story ends, but be missing the specifics, and when you get to the point where your story would end, you're still not sure how to end it.

This could be due to the main character not having evolved enough to be able to face the black moment and take the power they need to bring about the story's climax. If that is the case, I recommend examining your character carefully using the methods described above. After you're sure you understand him or her well enough, you should be able to determine what they need to have happen to them in order to be able to bring about the climax. Once you have that, you've got your course of action!

Another possible issue is that you haven't made up your mind about the ending itself. That is something you might have to figure out by outlining your novel, as I described in the previous chapter, and seeing what are the likely outcomes.

If the end itself is giving you anxiety, read on.

CHAPTER 6

THE END IS COMING... TOO SOON

You feel like the next logical step in your story is the end, but you're not ready for that yet. That can be paralyzing, and it's easy to see why you would shy away from the keyboard every time you have to write; you know it's coming, but you don't want it to come. There can be many reasons for that.

For starters, maybe you planned to write a full-length, 80k-word novel, only now you're barely 35k in and you've reached the climax, and now you can't write because this wasn't the way it was supposed to go. This one has a few different solutions:

You could accept that it's short. There's nothing wrong with that. You might have had your heart set on something longer, but sometimes it's better to accept that your story is shorter than to stuff it with endless filler and back story, which will bog down your plot. In the end, wouldn't you rather have readers who thought it was over too soon because they loved your story than readers who put it down half-finished because they got bored with it?

There are possible solutions if you absolutely need to lengthen your manuscript. However, it bears repeating that unless there are holes to fill in your story, you should try not to add anything to it; a tightly woven plot is much preferable to a higher word count. These solutions also involve revision of what is already written, so my suggestion is that you finish writing the plot you have in front of you, and then do any addition you would like to in the revision process.

If you do absolutely need to make your manuscript longer, one thing that you can do is re-examine your existing characters and see if you have explored all the tension, all the potential conflict that is inherent to them. Same with your plot: make sure everything is in place, everything is worked out; there may be opportunities to extrapolate on what you already have.

Another thing you can do if you want to lengthen is try to add sub-stories and secondary characters which enrich your main plot. You know how TV shows are structured so that in any given episode, there's one story about what the main characters are doing, another one that follows the secondary characters, and then a third, smaller one, that adds to the main, ongoing plotline of the season-wide arc? A lot of books are structured like that, too. See if you can't add new secondary characters with their own sub-stories. But be careful; this has to *enrich your main plot or further develop your main character*. It can't be random, or it's just filler, and we're back at the problem of having readers put down your book because they're bored with the filler.

If you've explored all these avenues and still feel the end is coming too quickly, or, on the contrary, the story is taking too long to reach its climax, then it is possible you have a pacing problem. This one is more related to form than it is to content itself, and I address it in part 2 of this book: it deserves a chapter of its own.

There are still more possible causes if you're blocking right at the end, though. Another possible problem is that you're not sure what the end *is*. If that is the problem, then you need to sit down and examine what you have established. It might help if you write up a quick outline of what you have so far so that you see the plot and subplots you have established and are able to wrap it all up neatly. If that doesn't help, you might want to sit and examine what your story is about, exactly. What is the idea behind it, and what would you like it to say? What position do you want to take on the subject matter? What do you want your characters' lives to be like when you're done with them? Do you want a happy outcome, or not? Asking yourself these questions should point you in the right direction.

You feel anxious about finishing this story, because you don't know or like what's next, or because you feel the climax is underwhelming. I am mentioning this one here because it can easily be mistaken as a problem of content, and maybe it even is. However, most of the time, it's a problem of confidence. I address problems of confidence in part 3 of this book. However, it *does* happen sometimes that the ending really isn't working. If you want to find out, I suggest showing it or talking about it with someone you trust to give you their honest opinion. If there really is a problem with the impact of your climax, then what I suggest is that you examine the *black moment* in your story, or the moment right before the climax when it feels like all hope is lost. Have you kicked your character hard enough? Have you brought them as far down as you can in the depths of despair? If you find that you can still hurt them a bit more at that moment, then doing so will decidedly help your climax hold more weight.

Chapter 7

You just can't write that next scene

It can happen sometimes that you come to a certain scene in the book that you don't feel like writing. It can feel natural to take a break then, but afterwards, when you try to get back to your project, you're facing that scene again, and you remember how much you don't feel like writing it, so you do something else.

If this keeps happening every time you're trying to get back in your story, that kind of block can be caused by quite a few things.

For starters, it could be a lack of confidence in your skill for writing a scene you consider difficult, or you're afraid to write it because it contains delicate subject matter, or it can be caused by you having lost enthusiasm for your story. These causes are actually *personal* causes, and are unrelated to your story; I cover these causes in part 3 of this book, so if that is what is bothering you, skip ahead there!

On the other hand, it could be because you have insufficient knowledge about one or more of the elements of your scene. If that is the case, I cover this in the very next chapter, so read on!

Finally, it could be that the next scene is simply not that exciting. If that is the case, then there might be a problem with the scene itself, and it may need to be changed, or removed entirely from the story. After all, if the scene is making you, the writer and the person most excited about this story, yawn and roll your eyes, imagine what the reader might think of it.

Examine what this scene contains. Does it provide information that is essential to the reader's comprehension of the plot or characters? No? Axe it. Yes? In that case, is it possible to take that information and include it in a more exciting scene which happens at some other point of the story, and axe the scene anyway?

If it isn't possible to remove the scene completely, you might want to look at what it is that is making it boring. Are the characters not doing anything else than having a mild conversation, which is heavy with exposition? If that is the case, then you might want to try changing things up a bit. Is it possible to add conflict to the discussion? Is there a character that could be present that really doesn't agree with what's going on? Or, possibly, could the characters be doing something at the same time, which makes having the conversation difficult, or dangerous? Is it possible to change the setting of the scene to one that is more engaging to the characters, somewhere that would provoke more actions and reactions? At any rate, if you find yourself struggling with a scene because it is much more boring than the rest of the scenes in your book, the best solution is to find a way to either remove it or to add conflict to it. As for how much conflict, it doesn't need to be end-of-the-world stuff; just enough so that you'll get excited about writing it again.

Chapter 8

You need more information

This problem is very similar to the previous one, but instead of having a piece of the story missing, you are missing a piece of knowledge that is hindering your ability to write that scene. A lot of the time, especially if you're a pantser rather than a planner, it's perfectly fine to do your research after having done the first draft, by noting the areas that need work and filling in the blanks when rewriting and revising. But sometimes, lack of knowledge is just too great, and can become crippling.

This can be technical knowledge. For example, if you are writing a mystery, and a scene is set at a police station, but you have no idea what a police station would look like, or what the booking procedure is, or where your character would go or what his rights are, that would be a very difficult scene to write.

It can also be related to world-building: if you are writing science-fiction, and only developed your aliens so far as to know what they look like, but nothing else. Then, when the first interactions happen between your characters and the aliens, it might *seem* obvious how the scene should go, but if you haven't given thought to their means of communication, their particular linguistics idiosyncrasies, their culture, their belief system, their societal values... all of those things come into play in any form of communication. Without knowing all of this, it can and will get extremely difficult to write a scene where the aliens interact with your characters.

This can also apply to characters and their backgrounds, too. It can be fun to go in blind, and throw in characters without knowing anything about them, hoping that they will grow and we will discover everything about them while writing, and honestly, that can go very well most of the time. Sometimes, though, the character doesn't progress well or can seem as though they are remaining flat and lifeless, or can be downright inconsistent in their replies. It's easy to get blocked in a deep conversational scene with a character we don't know that well yet, who suddenly needs to be saying profound things, when we're still not really sure who they are.

When confronted with a block that is due to lack of knowledge, there are two basic choices in front of you. The first is to skip the scene or part of the story that is posing the problem, and to go ahead with the rest of the story. That might seem like the easiest solution, and indeed it can really help if you're on a roll in your first draft and don't mind doing the extra work later. Because yes, it does mean extra work. If you skip a scene, especially because of lack of knowledge in a certain area, it could very well be that, after you've done your research or world-building or character creation, things happen in that scene a *very* different way than you had imagined before doing that. That will definitely have repercussions on the rest of the story, and might change small elements which will all have to be reworked during rewrites and edits. Those elements might, in turn, change other elements, like a ripple effect, so that you often end up having to make significant changes as a result of one skipped scene; often, this can end up being a lot more work than the alternative.

The second option would be to stop writing for the moment, and do what you need to do to get the information that you are missing to move forward. This can take the form of research, or of character development, using the methods described earlier in this book, or even of world building. I'm not going to get into what is required for world building in this volume, because entire books could be (and indeed have been) written on the subject. My website has quite a bit of information on how to do this well, if that is what you need. But the bottom line is, as daunting as this sounds right now, you will have to do this sooner or later, and I recommend doing it now rather than skipping a scene and having a lot of rewriting to do in the future.

PART 2

CAUSES RELATED TO FORM

The causes related to *form* are probably the most uncommon causes, but they do happen, and they are relatively easy to fix, even though they often demand a lot of work on what's already been written.

Causes related to form are very similar to those related to content. The main difference is that while content-related causes are something that's wrong with the story itself (or part of it), form-related causes are something that's wrong with the *way you're telling it.*

CHAPTER 9

NARRATIVE VOICE PROBLEMS

It can happen sometimes that you figure out halfway that you are using the wrong narrative voice.

Before I go any further, I just want to clarify something. There is an essential difference between narrative voice and point of view. A lot of people conflate the two, and that unfortunately leads to essentially misunderstanding both. This means not exploiting either to their full potential, or downright misusing both.

When you are deciding between 1st and 3rd person, you are choosing a narrative voice, NOT a point of view. The narrative voice is the way in which you tell your story; past or present tense, 1st, 2nd or 3rd person, etc. A point of view, on the other hand, represents *through which character's eyes* the reader will experience the story. While the chosen point of view will certainly influence the narrative voice you will end up using, they are two very different things, and should be considered with equal care. I will get into problems related to choice of point of view in the next chapter, because they are a few potential ones.

Why am I going on about this? Because when narrative voice is not understood, it can be easy to make a choice that might seem arbitrary at the beginning of your story, without really understanding its repercussions, and then get stuck later on because of the limitations inherent to some choices.

For example, first person can seem like a very natural choice for new authors, but it has a lot of limitations: it makes descriptions much more difficult to write well and fluidly, it can make exposition in narration seem awkward and forced, and, obviously, it limits the range of points of view you can express in a story.

By the way, it should be said that I am not saying it's wrong to use first person; I have, in fact, used many different voices myself. This is just an easy example. There are limitations with any narrative voice, which is why you should get to know all of them; it goes beyond simply choosing first and third person; there are *many* different kinds of narrative voice, and they each have things they do better and things they do poorly. You should choose the voice which fits what you need to do with your story.

So why am I going on about narrative voice? Well, if you find yourself stuck because you can't get a description right, or your exposition in narration feels stilted and awkward, or any other part of your story where you *know* what is happening but you just can't seem to get it *right...* you should try to see if you're using the right narrative voice. Try the scene in another voice, just to see if it might work out better. If it does, you might want to analyze whether this new voice would fit the rest of your book. It might demand a rewrite in that new voice, but you might discover new opportunities because of it.

You will find more information about narrative voice, on my website, carolinefrechette.com.

Chapter 10

Point of View Problems

A very closely related problem to the one of narrative voice is the choice of a (or many) point of view character for your story. With nearly every choice of narrative voice, you need to choose one character whose experience of the story will be the reader's. This might seem like an easy task, but it has to be a careful choice. You need to choose someone who will be there, at least as a witness, at the important moments in your story. You need to choose someone who knows enough about what is going on that the reader will be able to keep up with the story, but not too much as to give away everything too soon.

You can, of course, pick many different viewpoint characters for the same story, but you need to make sure you're using the right viewpoint at the right moment, and sometimes you can get a block even if you have many different characters, because you started a chapter with one character who suddenly isn't right for one scene inside your chapter; but more often than not, writer's block related to point of view characters happen when a story is told through a single viewpoint throughout.

For example, it can happen that you need to express or explain something that goes above, or outside of his or her realm of understanding, and you don't know how to do that. Or, you are having something important happen, and the character whose viewpoint you are following can't possibly be there. It can also happen that your character figures out some things that you don't want your reader to know yet... or, on the contrary, doesn't care enough about what's going on to figure things out or pay attention.

One obvious thing to do when you have the wrong viewpoint for a scene is to switch to a different point of view character. This is much more easily done if you have several viewpoint characters, but it is possible even if you have only one point of view character.

If you do have only one point of view character, then you should explore other solutions before you add a different viewpoint. This is especially true if you are writing in first person; alternating points of view in this narrative voice can be extremely hard to pull off. But even if you are working in third person, adding another viewpoint character in the middle of your story can be hard; it's usually inadvisable, for example, to have the entire book told in the point of view of one character, and then to jump to another one just for one scene. When you have a secondary viewpoint, it must be there consistently throughout your story.

So, before you try adding a secondary point of view to a story which only has one viewpoint character, you may want to try these things. If the character knows too much, is there a way to make the clue which provides him or her with the information more subtle? Or to have them distracted during this scene so that they don't immediately jump to conclusions?

If the problem is that you need to provide information about an event, or another character's feelings about a situation, is it possible to do this via dialogue and body language?

If all else fails, then you could add another viewpoint. But when you rewrite and revise, you will have to change certain scenes in the beginning to that particular viewpoint for the sake of consistency.

Chapter 11

Pacing problems

Pacing problems can be difficult to diagnose and solve, and they are part content-related, and part form-related. There isn't a universal rule that stories should be paced a certain way; in fact, certain stories demand a faster pace, like adventure stories, thrillers, and other action-driven stories, and some demand a much slower pace, such as fantasy epics, and highly psychological stories.

That being said, having the wrong pace in your story can cause a block, for example when you feel a story is going too fast and you reach the climax too soon, you might have a hard time reaching the climax because you haven't fleshed out the rest of the story enough, and the emotional impact might not be there. If that is the case, then you can try going back from the beginning and fleshing out the story as much as you can, until your character's emotional journeys carry you naturally to the climax.

On the contrary, sometimes it can happen that the pace is much too slow for the kind of story you're telling, and you're constantly finding yourself bored with what you're writing, or you're 75k words in and you haven't even reached the middle of your story. If you haven't done an outline, it may be a sign that you need to do one; when working without an outline, it can happen that we move from one action to the next, without taking breaks, so that the story ends up filled with scenes that don't move the plot forward or build character. Fortunately, you don't have to go back and fix this immediately, though you will need to do so when editing. However, doing an outline for the rest of the story might help you keep to the scenes which are essential, and help you move forward.

Another thing that might help if your pace is too slow is to try and skip ahead to the important scenes in your book, and write the scenes out of order, much like you would an outline. This will definitely help keep out any unnecessary scenes, though it might mean a little bit more work when you get to rewriting.

Chapter 12

Tone problems

Another area where it is crucially important to maintain consistency is the tone of your book. Tone is what makes a reader decide whether or not he or she is in the mood to keep reading the story, so it's important to establish something that remains constant throughout the book.

When you come to a scene that needs to break away from the overall mood of your book, it can seem like it's coming out all wrong, because you suddenly need to write in a tone which has been drastically different than what you have been writing so far. You might feel that you're doing it poorly because you don't know how to make it fit with your current narrative voice, which is perfect for the main tone of your book, and it's causing you to be unable to move forward.

For example, you're writing a light-hearted comedy, but you need to include someone dying. Or you're writing a very dark horror piece, and you need to write the part where the two main characters realize their love for one another.

This is not so much a problem to solve as it is a "handle with care" situation; you need to proceed differently than you usually would. The trick to writing a scene that has a very different mood from the rest of your book while remaining consistent with tone is that you need to blend the two tones (the scene and the overall story).

This is delicate, but I find that a good way to do this is to write it in the tone in which the scene comes most naturally, even if you know that it won't be right for your story, and to then modify it to make it a little more like the other tone. This can appear like a waste of time if you're a die-hard planner, but the truth is, if you're sitting in front of your computer playing *Angry Birds* instead of writing, you're wasting time anyway, so you might as well do something constructive.

So give yourself permission to write something that might not fit but that will be there to revise later; it's always preferable to have that than nothing at all. Once the scene is written, then all you have to do is tweak it to add overtones of your story's mood, and that can be done in revision.

CHAPTER 13

DESCRIPTION PROBLEMS

Another very common form problem which stumps a lot of people is writing descriptions. Some people love to do it and have no problems doing so, but for others, it feels like pulling teeth, every time. If you're among the latter, chances are you have experienced getting blocked while trying to write a description at least once.

If you're stuck because you know there should be a description in your story at the moment you're at but you just can't write it, then simply don't write it. Skip it and get back to the action. It's perfectly okay to not respect a plan perfectly. You could make a note in your manuscript that you mean to add a description here later, and do it when you revise. After all, descriptions don't change anything to the events of your story, so you can absolutely add them in later without it changing anything to the rest of your story.

UNBLOCKED

You may even find that you don't even need a description there, when you get to the revision. Often, if something feels forced, or not right, it can mean that maybe it doesn't flow well with the pace of the story, and that it isn't at its proper place where you want it to be. Don't try to force something that doesn't come naturally. Sometimes it just doesn't belong.

Part 3

Personal Causes

Sometimes, there's absolutely nothing wrong with your story, or with the way you're telling it, but you still feel unable to write every time you try, or it seems much more difficult than it used to be, and it happens no matter what you're trying to work on. If this is the case, then you might have a *personal* problem.

Personal problems as I discuss them here cover everything that is related to your person and not your story, like your physical health, your work environment, your mental state, or even how you process new story ideas. There are almost as many personal causes as there are causes related to form and content put together, and although some of them have easy enough answers, some are a bit more complicated to solve.

Whether or not they have easy solutions, writer's block that is due to personal reasons is even more important to examine carefully. While content and form reasons might eventually become obvious if you put the work down and come back to it later, writer's block that is caused by personal reasons is likely to get worse if ignored, and won't respond to the many well-meaning suggestions of how to generate ideas. Furthermore, the inability to write itself might make the issues causing the block to get worse, so it makes it essential to get to the root of the problem.

Chapter 14

Loss of enthusiasm about the story

Sometimes, there's nothing wrong with your story, but you still feel bored with your project. You try and pick it up but roll your eyes and sigh every time you look at the place you're at. You've lost all the enthusiasm you had for this project when you first started it.

There are actually a few things you can do in order to try to rekindle enthusiasm for your project. Talking about it with someone you trust and who knows your story might help you find what it was that so excited you about this project in the first place. Not only that, but the people you speak to might show enough interest or enthusiasm to breathe it back into you.

Another thing you could try, and one of my favorites when this happens to me, would be to re-read your story from the beginning. Take what you've written so far, go somewhere comfortable where you like to read, and read it. From the beginning. Not like a writer, not doing any revision, just reading it. Enjoying it. After all, if you once were excited about this project enough to work on it, reading this story should be enjoyable. What will happen, most often, is that you will get to the point where you are at, and want the story to go on.

Character interviews are something else you could try. I explain how to do those on my website, and in Chapter 5 of this book. Sometimes, especially if you are character driven, sitting down and spending some time with the people who are the reason you decided to write this story to begin with might rekindle the flame, as it were.

If all else fails, then the only solution might be to put aside the project and work on something else. I know, I said that by reading this book you would kick writer's block for sure. But if you've completely fallen out of love with a project, and nothing can bring it back, then it's okay to put it aside and work on something else. It doesn't mean that you have writer's block. The problem isn't with you, or even the project itself, it's about the relationship between you two. If it was meant to be, then eventually you'll be driven to pick it up again and you'll get it done then. But trying to force yourself to write something you just have lost any and all excitement for is not necessarily productive. In fact, it can be quite counter-productive, as it may well be preventing you from getting other work done, and will fuel your sense of writer's block until it morphs into something more serious.

Chapter 15

Too many new ideas

Sometimes, what happens isn't that we get bored with our story, but rather we keep having new ideas that are more interesting than what we are writing at the moment. If that happens to you, then you might think you have writer's block and can't get very far into a story because you keep putting your stories down to start new ones. This is what I call "the starting bug."

It's perfectly normal to do that, and you would probably be surprised at just how many people go through the exact same thing. After all, it's extremely exciting to begin a new project. A new idea invariably sparks creativity and interest in a project, and that excitement might dwarf the one you feel for the project you're working on. However, the appeal of the new idea doesn't necessarily come from the fact that the new idea is more complete, better, or readier to be written. The truth is, in most cases, that it is the newness of it which is exciting, exactly like a new toy, and not the nature of the new idea.

I'm just going to take a moment to explain why it's very important to see our stories through. It might seem like it's no big deal, but if you're doing that all the time, there are other issues that can arise besides the kind of writer's block it can cause.

First of all, there is nothing like actually finishing a novel to truly learn about the kind of writing which works for you. More importantly, if you never finish a story, how will you ever publish anything? Most important of all, although starting a new story can be extremely exciting, the best part of any story is the (aptly named) climax. Think about it this way. Writing only the beginning of a story before putting it aside to start another is exactly like starting a relationship with someone, and immediately dumping them for someone who seems more attractive, over and over again. If you do that with your relationships, you'll always be living the thrill of new love, but you'll never get to enjoy the really good parts. After all, the best parts of a relationship only happen when you've gotten to truly know someone, and they've truly gotten to know you; when you've established an ease with each other. The same goes for your story: you get the most enjoyment from it once you really get to know it, and you see it in all its depth.

There are a few things you can do to help yourself if this is your problem. First, if you're afraid of losing your new idea, keep an ideas log. This is like a journal, in which you write every idea you have, and elaborate on them as much as you want to without actually writing the story itself. It can be in the shape of a notebook, or a binder where you can write on loose-leaf paper and group all your story notes together. You can even do that on the computer, starting a new Word document for every new story.

There is a very good reason to note your ideas without starting a new project right away; ideas need to mature, to grow, and you need to give them that space. If you write them down in a journal, they can go rest on the back burner where they need to be until they are ripe enough to live up to their potential.

Something I do myself because I have so many ideas is to work on several projects at once. Usually I will be writing one or two first drafts at a time, and revising or rewriting at least one other project. Being able to rotate between tasks prevents boredom to set in, and when I feel sick of working on something I can just move to something else for a little while. If you feel like you absolutely *have* to get writing on a project right away, maybe this could be something to consider. You could start the new project, and keep writing the one you are working on.

When this happens to me, I usually establish a kind of rewards system with the new story. Every day, I get to write the new story only if I have reached a minimum word count in my current project. This serves to motivate me to get those words down, and fast, because I want to get to that story I'm excited about. It's extremely efficient for boosting output, because on top of riding the thrill of writing the new story, I have additional motivation for writing my ongoing project.

Lastly, I suggest reading the previous chapter about how to fall back in love with the story you're currently working on. Maybe you can get back the excitement that you felt when you first started writing it!

Chapter 16

The wrong environment

Another thing that can really look like writer's block is *writing in the wrong environment*. Writing is a highly intellectual activity, and writing in the wrong environment can have a hugely negative impact on your output. If you're always trying to write in the same environment, it can really feel like the problem is coming from you, or from your story.

A lot of people will tell you what you absolutely must do when it comes to choosing an environment to write in. They might say that silence is golden, that isolation is key, or that you must have music that fits the mood of your book. As with everything, and especially when it comes to choosing the right environment, the only absolute is what works for *you*.

When considering whether or not these things work for you, don't just go by your impression. You should try measuring word count of your productive period, and see which one yields the best results.

Unblocked

The first thing you have to think about is people. Some writers function really well in an environment where there are a lot of people. They like the camaraderie, being able to take breaks and talk, etc. Others cannot function at all when others are present; they get distracted by people-watching, or spend all their time talking and can barely write. Having people around, whether you know them or not, can be a great help, or it can be a great distraction. So find out what works best for you! It might be great to go to writer's circles and coffee shops, or it might be what has you blocked.

Sounds often go hand in hand with the presence of others. For example, some writers swear by writing to music. It can be awesome to put you in the mood, give you a sort of soundtrack to keep you concentrated on your story. However, there are many people, some of whom might enjoy listening to music while they write, for whom music might be a distraction. If you find yourself paying attention to the music you are listening to, closing your eyes to listen to some passages, it might be that you need to at least try silence. Several studies demonstrate that listening to music stimulates the same areas of the brain as eyesight does, and that when you are surrounded by noise or listening to music, you might be less able to notice details about your environment, or to pay attention to your text. So give silence a try, just to see whether or not it helps your productivity!

One word about the TV: if you *must* have it on as background noise, you should sit facing away from the screen. Listening is one thing... when you're looking at it too, then writing isn't getting done.

Lights are another thing that people seldom think about as being an important part of their environment. Lights can have a huge impact on your ability to write. And I'm not just talking about insufficient light if you're using a notebook, either (though if that's your case, then I definitely recommend an adjustment). Having a source of light above your screen, for example, like a window through which the sun is shining, or a bright lamp, it might cause you to have to lean down so your eyes are closer to your screen. This can lead to neck pain, which can hurt your concentration. Make sure that lighting is appropriate, not too strong and not too dim, so that you're not having to change your position because of it.

Finally, ergonomics is something else that you should keep in mind if you're having trouble concentrating on your writing. Is your back in the right position? Are your legs? What about your neck and head? Your elbows and wrists? Take some time and research what a truly ergonomic position should be like, and try to change your environment accordingly. Pain and discomfort can be a huge factor in the ability to write, as we'll see in the next chapter. I have provided links in the ***Resources*** section of this book.

Chapter 17

Taking care of your body

It should go without saying, but the first thing you need to pay attention to is your own body. I'm definitely not saying you need to be an athlete to be able to write, but if something is wrong with your body, it might severely impede your ability to perform in all the areas of your life, including writing.

If you buy a brand new car, it'll run great; but after a little while, if you never take it in to change the oil and do preventative maintenance, eventually it'll break down and stop working. The problem won't be the road you're driving on, or the trip you're taking; it's your car that won't run. So no matter how long and carefully you planned the trip, you might be unable to take that first step because you neglected your vehicle.

Writing is a very lonely, sedentary lifestyle. On top of that, if you're anything like me, you probably find it easy to get completely wrapped up in your work and forget to eat or sleep or even go to the bathroom for much too long, not to mention paying attention to aches and pains and getting very little exercise. It can be much easier than you might think to stop taking care of ourselves, because, after all, it's the mind that does the work when you write, isn't it? Well, your brain starts seriously lagging when it's not properly rested, fed and hydrated. Issues affecting your body can cause you to have a very hard time concentrating, which might, in turn make it seem like you just can't write (or can't write anything good if you're managing to get the words out). If you're having a hard time writing, but have no idea why that is, you might want to examine how you physically feel, and whether there is something you can do to make yourself feel better.

Go see your doctor regularly, go get your teeth cleaned at the dentist's, make sure you get an eye exam at least once every few years, eat healthy food three times a day, and go to bed at a reasonable hour, or an hour that lets you sleep a full night. Also make sure that you are minimally active, and that if you are experiencing pain or weird symptoms, that you see a medical professional about it right away.

Chapter 18

Knowing your natural cycle

As with the previous chapter, it can happen sometimes that you have trouble getting started or producing anything, but you are perfectly healthy. If that is your case, you might want to examine if you're on the right schedule. That can mean your sleep schedule, yes, but most of the time, it means that your writing schedule might be off too. And if you're thinking, "well I don't have a writing schedule," please keep reading. Just because you don't write it down on paper or even set aside time to write doesn't mean you're not affected by your creative schedule.

Everyone has their own best sleeping schedule. Some people do best when they sleep one stretch of sleep, but the exact length varies from person to person. Some do best with six hours of sleep, and others need at least ten. Some absolutely need to be in bed by 9:00 PM, and others do fine if they go to bed at 1:00 or 2:00 AM. Some people even sleep better if they do it in two shorter stretches, sometimes two stretches in the night, and sometimes a few hours at night with an afternoon nap. It's imperative, especially if you have a tendency to feel tired for no reason, that you find which sleep schedule fits you best, so that you are at your best when it comes to concentration.

But what I really want to discuss in this chapter is your productivity peak. Everyone has a moment in the day (or night) when they are the most productive. It can happen, however, that this moment is not the one we think it is, especially because it tends to change over time.

For example, when I was a teenager, my most productive moments, writing-wise, were very late at night, until 2:00 or 3:00 AM. When I hit my mid-twenties, I found that I wasn't nearly as productive as I used to be. I thought there was something wrong with me, until I tried writing early in the morning, and the words just poured out. Next day, same thing again, and the day after that… it seemed my natural peak productive hour had shifted from late night to early morning, all by itself. I got into the habit of getting up early and getting my writing done before anything else in the day. And then, I hit my mid-thirties and had my second child, and it wasn't working anymore. I just couldn't produce. I thought for sure, it must be the exhaustion, but one sleepless night, I picked up my writing again, and there it was: my peak hours had flipped back to the middle of the night. A bit impractical with two young kids who get up around six, but it is what it is: I get more done between 1:00 and 3:00 AM than I do in four or five hours if I try to write at another time.

So if it hasn't been working for a while, for you, try another time of day. Try it during your lunch hour, or right after dinner, or after the kids are in bed. Try it as you're having breakfast. Try going to bed at 1:00 or 2:00 AM and seeing if it works better there, and try it late in the afternoon before making dinner. The only way you will figure out what your peak hour is will be to try many different times. You'll have to do it every few years, too, since just because you find it once doesn't mean it'll stay the same! As your life changes, so does your peak hour, so keep making sure you're working at the best time for you.

Chapter 19

What will my mother think?

A lot of personal reasons have to do with fear. I will go over some of the common ones in the chapters of this book, which deal with self-esteem and fear of failure, but I wanted to address this fear-related issue by itself, because it is a very common one: self-censorship.

When we write things we are very passionate about, we tend to draw from our innermost feelings, the thoughts and emotions which define us, which we hold most dear. These thoughts and emotions can sometimes feel scary to face, and then write, not only because they are so personal, but also because they often stem from the most traumatizing experiences we have been through.

The main reason that most people hesitate to write what is truly preoccupying to them is that they are afraid of facing those feelings. Not exactly of having them, since obviously, they already have them if they're feeling this way: what they are afraid of is that if they put the feelings into words, it makes them *real,* whereas if they don't talk about them or face them they can ignore the fact that they are there. This fear is one of the hardest to deal with, because it is often subconscious. It's irrational, too; the fact that you have these feelings makes them real, not the fact that you write them down or talk about them. When you do write about them, you finally allow yourself to start making peace with those feelings. It doesn't make them more or less real, but it does make you more likely to accept them, and yourself, in the process.

Another common self-censorship fear is what others will think if they find out that this is what you have in your heart. This one is both easier and harder to deal with than the other types of fear. The truth is, no matter what you write, your friends and family will look at your stories and try to find all sorts of reflections of your life in them. They will interpret and analyze and wonder, and the only thing you can do to prevent them from doing it is not write at all. You'll be surprised at the number of things they think you've taken from your life, or the characters they think you've modeled after them. So, if they're going to do it anyway, why not write down the things that really matter to you? Your answer will be the same then as it would be if they were making connections that aren't really there: it's fiction!

You might also be surprised by how much they *don't* think that you have based anything on your life, or how much they focus on the positive rather than the negative. I spent years fighting the urge to write my own series, *Family by Choice*, because it deals with abuse, anger, and violence, and I wasn't ready for my mother to read these things and know that I was dealing with those demons. I was shocked when I learned that my mother had not only devoured the books, but had also loved them. What I failed to realize was that my story also dealt with love, support systems, and healing, and that *this* was what was important to the story, and what readers took from it.

One extremely good reason, besides everything I've said so far, to acknowledge those feelings and write about them, is that they'll come through in your writing whether you try to suppress them or not; but if you never own up to them, you'll never be able to move past them to explore other feelings that might make a good basis for a story. You'll also end up with a pattern to your stories, with something in particular coming up over and over again, and they might get repetitive. Of course, it's all right if you keep exploring those feelings, but if you do it consciously, you'll have a much better chance at finding original ways to do it instead of writing the same story with different characters and settings every time.

Chapter 20

Writing Life Blues

It can happen that we feel low, depressed, and no matter what, we can't seem to get out of that funk. Sometimes, it can be something serious, like depression, or a crippling self-doubt that you have been carrying for years and runs much deeper than your ability to write. I deal with those in the last three chapters of this book.

Sometimes, though, you're just discouraged with being a writer, or you're having a bad week. There are things to do to spring back from that.

If you've just gotten a scathing review, or your 42nd rejection letter, or a really harsh critique from your group or one of your beta readers, or your mom has shared yet another article with you about how writers make no money and asked "when are you going to get a *real* job, honey?", it could very well be that you're just suffering from market blues. You can feel like you're a hack, like writing is a waste of time, or like you're never going to make it or be any good, so why bother?

That can be paralyzing. After all, how are you going to perform well doing a task that you are currently convinced that you are incapable of doing, and serves no purpose anyway? By the way, it should be said that this happens to all of us, at every stage of our career. The solution to this is take a break from your writing to do these things. First, try to sit with yourself and remember why you write. Write it down, either in your ideas journal or on a sheet or paper you can put in a binder and pull out when you need to remember, or even something you can put up on your wall as an affirmation. It might seem silly to do, but it's actually extremely important: after all, chances are that you write because you need to tell your stories, not for some external validation like money or admiration, and it's good to be reminded that you do it for yourself when outside sources discourage you.

Another thing you might do is hang out with your fans. Don't say anything about getting a bad review; just go to a place where you know your work is loved. A few authors I know have Facebook groups where their fans meet and discuss their books. Just going through posts in those groups can cheer you up, or even posting a "what is your favorite scene?" thread. If you have yet to publish, why not turn to the beta readers who have loved your book and ask them to talk about their favorite bits? If you're reeling from a bad review, you could always go and look back at the positive ones you've gotten, or even look up your favorite book or author on Goodreads or Amazon and looking at the bad reviews *they* got. That should show you beyond a doubt that reviews are subjective, and just because someone didn't like a book doesn't mean they're right or that their opinion is even universal.

If you're suffering from rejection blues, try Googling "famous author rejections." Rejections are part of a writer's life, and they're especially common in this day and age. Seeing that some of your favorite authors went through the same thing (and they all did) might definitely make you feel better.

If you're still feeling insecure about your story, it's ok to put it aside and work on something else for the time being. If you don't think you can do it, then you might be having deeper self-esteem issues, and I encourage you to read the chapters of this book dedicated to self-esteem and fear of failure, which might be more help to you.

Chapter 21

Real life is taking over

Life isn't kind, and as writers (or professional torturers of characters) we know this better than most. Often, it becomes impossible to write because our heads are filled with the fight we had with our significant other, our work schedule being changed for the worst, a natural disaster that destroyed part of our home, or the government suddenly recalculating our taxes and deciding we owe them thousands of dollars… anything can happen, and thoughts of our problems can get invasive to the point of not allowing anything else in. When this happens, it can seem impossible to concentrate on what you're writing. This can feel like writer's block, but really, you're not blocked, you're just preoccupied.

This one is tough to get over, and there aren't many solutions. The only thing you can do is try to compartmentalize, to push those invading thoughts out of your mind so you can write. After all, thinking about the problems you can't deal with right away is something that is disruptive and completely counter-productive; if you can't do anything about it at the moment, you might as well not be stressing out over it.

If this sounds easier said than done, it's because it is. It's incredibly hard to push away intrusive thoughts, but it can be done with practice. One technique is to try to have an object or image that you can use to "ground" yourself, to bring your thoughts back into the positive. It can be an inspirational quote, a picture that reminds you of a happy event in your life, anything positive that you can focus your thoughts on. I know it sounds hard, but it is possible to get yourself back in the mindset you need to be, as long as you feed your thoughts the right kind of information.

Another thing you can do is change your environment. If you are ok with writing surrounded by people, go in a coffee shop, a pub, or another public place where you know you might run into people you know. If you prefer silence, go to the library, or the park, anywhere you can sit down and write. A change of setting is often all you need to get your mind off of your problems for a little while.

Finally, if all else fails, try doing some physical exercises. Going out for a jog, or a bike ride, or a swim, can really take your mind off of things. Also, there are a few very effective relaxation techniques (link in the ***Resources*** section) which you can try, that can help center you on yourself. Also, feel free to take a little break. Watch a movie. Read a bit. Play a video game. *Change your mind.* When you're feeling better, you'll be able to jump right back into your writing and keep the thoughts at bay until they need to be addressed.

Chapter 22

Poor self-esteem

Sometimes, the fears we have related to writing run much deeper than simple self-censorship. It's not just about *this* story, and *this* issue, but it manifests itself when you're trying to write *any* story at all. A way to identify this is if you're doing self-sabotage or extensive avoidance that translates into procrastination, even if that procrastination is doing research or learning or anything else that's not writing.

I've known many writers who couldn't finish anything, or who couldn't even start putting words down because they were systematically dissatisfied with what they were writing. They compared themselves to their favorite authors, and found that their writing was not as good. Or, they just thought they couldn't do it, that they would never be any good, which prevented them from even finding out if they were good or not, because they had been so paralyzed by those feelings that they couldn't write anything at all.

Then, there is also fear of failure which is at play in all this; you can become so convinced that you are bound to fail that you don't dare try anything because of the risk of failure. I will address this one in the next chapter, and keep this one about crippling self-criticism which is the result of poor self-esteem.

First, let me tell you that you should never compare yourself to other writers. It's great, and very necessary, to read as much as you can, but the purpose of this is not comparison. To begin with, many of the authors you will read are very experienced, so if you are writing your very first book, it's not only likely, but expected that your style won't be as established and confident as theirs. Also, what you have in your hands is definitely *not* a first draft, so why should you be comparing what you produce in your first draft to it?

With that being said, here are a few tips to help get past those fears. Begin by telling yourself that you will never, EVER show this to anyone. Save it on a USB key instead of your hard drive. Put that key, or your notebook, in a safe, under a loose board in the attic floor, or under your fridge; some place that no one else will think of. Create a secret email account so you can email it to yourself, and no one else can see it. Password-protect everything. Do anything that will make you feel better and reassure you that no one else can see it. When you're done, you can decide if you want to show it or destroy it, but for now, don't worry about it. If you need encouragement, you can make yourself a fake Facebook profile, an alias, and get encouragement from a writing community that never has to find out who you are. There are even online critique groups you can join. Anonymity can be reassuring to the anxious mind.

As for self-criticism, and disliking everything you come up with, why not make it a challenge? Dare yourself. Write poorly... on purpose. You will almost always be surprised by what you come up with when you give yourself permission to write poorly. Give yourself permission to try. Have fun with it! Something that I do with my first drafts is that when I write something I violently dislike, I write myself a comment in parenthesis next to it. It can be anything from a pertinent, calm comment about what I dislike in the passage, to a rant in all caps about how bad it is (which very often contains the word "ugh"). And if you're that much of a perfectionist that it needs to be perfect, well, that's what revision is for. If you write something that's "perfect" right away, you'll be skipping an essential part of the process. So please, write that bad part. See it as building a foundation to grow on, which is what a first draft really is. And before you start revising... *finish your novel*. You need to have the whole picture before you can make changes to all its parts; that's how you end up with a cohesive whole.

Chapter 23

Fear of failure

Another common fear is failure. You may be afraid to start at all, because you're so afraid that you will fail. First of all, let me tell you that "failure" is not a static state; it's not something that can be an end result of anything, unless you stop writing. Failure is just a stepping stone to achievement.

Failure happens to be part of everything we attempt. It has to be. If there wasn't such a thing as "trial and error", we wouldn't discover new things, we would never advance in any field whatsoever, and we wouldn't be able to learn; to be confident in what works, we have to experience what doesn't. Pablo Picasso said it best: "I am always doing that which I cannot do, in order that I may learn to do it."

That goes double, triple, quadruple, and a hundredfold when creating art. Art is a subjective pursuit, in which there is no set end result; as Leonardo Da Vinci said, "Art is never finished; only abandoned." In fact, the very process, the journey to the finished piece is itself as important, sometimes even more so, than the end result itself. If not for failure, art would be impossible. It is mistakes and unintended results that often lead the way to true innovation, to the greatest ideas, and to new techniques.

This doesn't just apply to visual art. Every artist – be it actor, painter, illustrator, sculptor, musician, and writer – must learn to venture outside of their comfort zone to progress in their art. That is how they test their limits and discover that they are capable of so much more. And, by the way, "testing your limits" doesn't mean you succeed the first time you try something outside of your comfort zone; in fact, if you do succeed right away, chances are you haven't really reached one of your limits yet. It takes trying over and over again to be able to push back these boundaries and add another skill to your toolset.

Writers and composers have such a huge advantage over other artists in that respect. When creating visual art and you try something that doesn't work, more often than not you will have to scrap that drawing, or paint over that canvas, or throw away that sculpture. You have to start all over again until you find the one that works. When you're writing, though, no matter what new thing you're trying, you'll very, very rarely have to scrap everything and start all over again. Once you've got that first draft down, you can tweak it, change it, edit it until it's finally the way you want it. You have so, so much more luxury to make mistakes than most other artists. Take advantage of it. Let loose with that first draft. Give yourself permission to fail, to write something really bad. Stop letting fear of not writing a sentence perfectly the first time around make you stare blankly at your screen for an hour. Let it be a bad sentence. You can go back and fix it once you've written all the rest of your sentences. Chances are high anyway that you'll have a much better idea of the voice you want to give this project by the end, and then it's so much easier to go back and correct it with that in mind.

A friend of mine used to say that even if you fall flat on your face... depending on your height, you're more or less five feet closer than you were the moment before. The only true failure happens when you decide not to get up again. When you stop trying. The minute you're not doing something that leads you to make some mistakes... you've stopped getting better at what you do. So continue to celebrate your successes, by all means.

But also learn to celebrate your mistakes; they mean you're getting better.

Chapter 24

Mental health issues

Sometimes, it's more than just a temporary setback, and it's more than writing life blues. Mental health issues can be absolutely crippling to a writer, and it's often the one that is the hardest to identify and find a solution to.

Entire books, or, more accurately, entire libraries have been written on how to deal with these issues, and it sometimes can take many years to get past them. But there are a few things which you can do to help yourself write, even if you suffer from mental health issues, and I think a good way to do that is to tackle these issues in your writing, in a way that can help you heal. (N.B.: writing, while still a form of therapy, should not be the only thing you use as therapy. If you are suffering from a mental health issue, my recommendation is that you see a professional, in addition to these tips.)

Stories are basically about emotions; yes, they often have intelligent plots and raise subversive questions, but in the end, they make most of their points emotionally, because that is the way they have the most impact. If you want to make sure your stories impact your reader, you are going to have to delve in your deepest emotions, the ones that matter most to you, the ones that are at the core of your very being. That usually means confronting the things that are difficult for you to look at and deal with in your life, with the things that you've kept hidden at the bottom of yourself forever. Most of the time, though not always, this means tackling bad experiences and their aftermath, and though it's never easy, it's always liberating and leads to truly compelling writing.

So how do you know what to write about? How do you know what truly matters to you? Well, that's simple, and it's not. It's simple, because you know. Deep down, you know what makes you emotional, what makes you angry beyond all reason, what makes you go overboard; if it makes you more emotional or angry than most people around you, then it's something that truly matters to you and you alone, and you know you've touched one of your chords. The trick is to find a calm moment to try and identify these feelings, to look back at your behavior and see what provoked it, to see what it is exactly in your life, and in your experience that compares to whatever it was that triggered the emotion, and you'll have something that truly matters to you.

What it really takes is courage and introspection. Most people will spend a lot of their life running from their strongest emotions, their deepest hurt, afraid that they are not able to face them. Truly looking at oneself in the mirror is not for the faint of heart; but then again, neither is writing. Besides, true introspection is one of the essentials you must master to learn empathy and character creation.

This is, of course, easier said than done. Mental illnesses can be crippling, not just to your writing, but to your day to day life. They are also unfortunately still considered taboo, and a lot of people still fear discussing or even disclosing their issues to others. This can lead not only to a block because of self-censorship, but it can also leave you feeling isolated and unheard, which can often lead to these conditions to worsen. As far censorship is concerned, I recommend reading the chapter I wrote about it a bit earlier in the book. But I will add this: talking about these feelings, especially in a way that leads to healing, might help some of your readers in ways you can't imagine. What better reason could there be to eliminate self-censorship?

In addition of self-censorship, there is also a more insidious fear, which is that of what lies afterwards when you finally let go of these feelings. Sometimes, we feel so bad for so long that it's hard to imagine that there is life beyond the hurt, and you may be afraid that if you let go of the hurt, you will have nothing left of who you are. Well, that simply isn't true. While it is true that some experiences leave us changed forever, you are still someone after they've happened, if maybe not exactly the same person that you were before. But isn't it possible that this new person that you are is bigger, stronger and better for having been through those experiences?

These experiences, these feelings, are part of who you are. Learning to embrace and accept them is essential to learn to embrace and accept yourself. You will never be at your creative best as long as you do not do this. Besides, you might as well; you're stuck with you for the rest of your life, so why not learn to love yourself?

Some things happen in life that are truly horrible, make no sense, and are completely unfair. That's life, and it happens to everyone, to varying degrees. These things can sometimes cause great wounds in the mind and spirit, wounds that we have to learn to heal because though sometimes time helps, it doesn't always do the trick all by itself. Many things can help, and writing is one of them. Besides which, writing about a bad experience doesn't just help you, but it can help others, too, who have gone through similar experiences. After all, statistically speaking, if it's happened to you, chances are high that it's happened to many other people in different ways.

HOW TO MAKE WRITING TRULY THERAPEUTIC

There are many ways to write about things that make us feel emotional, about things that have really hurt us in our lives. You have to be careful, though: there are ways that heal, and others which keep the wound open and makes it fester.

First of all, when something bad happens, give yourself a little time to grieve before you write about it. It's no use if the wound is too fresh; you need to let the dust settle first.

Second, although our first impulse is going to be writing about what happened, that is a mistake. Writing about the events only bring them to memory, and makes us go through them again; you can end up making things worse than they were this way. What you have left from those events, what you have to deal with now, is the *emotional aftermath*; that is what you need to write about, because that is what you need to make sense of. What is done is done, and what has happened has happened, and it's over now; but you still carry the wounds of that time, and those are what you need to tend to.

Acceptance is a hard stage to reach, because we need to face our anger and pain. It's also hard because it can feel like because we finally accept what happened, it makes it okay. Well, it doesn't. What happened was wrong, but it happened, and no amount of anger can change that. That is what you need to accept. It happened.

Writing out exactly what happened is tempting, but mostly it stirs up more anger and pain, and it pulls us backwards in the grieving process. If this happens, try to find a way to keep yourself grounded in the present. Talk to a trusted loved one. Step away from your writing for a while. Take a bath. Eat some cake. And before you tackle your writing again, ask yourself if you're really writing about the emotional aftermath, or if you're rehashing what happened and trying to make sense of it. Remember: it might never make sense because life simply doesn't make sense sometimes, and there's no use dwelling on it.

Science-fiction writer J. Michael Straczynski wrote something that expresses my thoughts on this very well:

> *I used to think it was awful that life was so unfair. Then I thought, 'wouldn't it be much worse if life were fair, and all the terrible things that happen to us come because we actually deserve them?' So now I take great comfort in the general hostility and unfairness of the universe.*
> – Marcus Cole, *Babylon 5*

So if you're not supposed to re-live the events, how do you write about your emotions, then?

I've found that the best way to write about pain and hurt is through your characters. Your characters are usually strong and resilient; they have reserves of strength that make them able to get through the difficulties of the plot. This is the best way you can deal with your pain: *give it to them.*

Give them the things that went wrong in your life, the things you are hoping to get through; make it their background. Break them before the beginning, and then make them go through the story. They may be able to say the things you can't; they will certainly have the flaws you don't like in yourself because of what happened.

But in writing them through your story, you will also discover the strength they have because of what happened. How it improved their character and made them stronger, greater, kinder, more generous, and altruistic. When you see how loved they can be despite their flaws and their wounds, when you see how they took what life dealt to them and used it to become better people, you will realize that you can do the same as well. In fact, you probably have done the same and never realized it, since you are able to write these characters!

By taking them through the emotional journey they need to reach acceptance, you can get there yourself, and the best part about being a writer is you can do it as many times, with as many characters and as many different situations as you need.

Acknowledgements

Creative writing has always been a passion of mine, and when I started learning how to do it, through a combination of research, teachers, and lots and lots of practice, I discovered that I loved to not only do it, but also talk about it. When people around me started manifesting the need for help with writing theory, and I decided to "whip up a little something", I realized I had accumulated enough to teach a full-fledged class about writing. I've now been teaching creative writing and coaching writers for over a decade, and I love it.

My students have taught me as much about teaching as I have taught them about writing, and for that, I'm intensely grateful. The more I teach, the more I learn, and the broader my mind becomes, and for that, the people to whom I owe the most gratitude for this book are all the people whom I've ever taught, everyone who has ever manifested a need to beat an obstacle in their writing. To my creative writing students, in particular, thank you.

I also would love to thank my good friend Phil: you're the one who started me down that road all those years ago, and without you, I wouldn't be anywhere near where I am right now. Thank you.

Thanks also go to my friend Kevin Johns; you are so generous of your time and knowledge, and you have made so many things possible for me and my career. I'm glad to have met you. You're a rare species indeed: a genuine, honest-to-goodness good guy, with more kindness in your heart than you know. Thank you.

As always, a big thank-you to my critique group members: Marie-Claude, Marjolaine, Amy, Eric, Manon, Jessica. You may not have directly participated in this one, but our many discussions have helped made it what it is.

Finally, a big thank you to the team at Renaissance, especially L. P. Vallée and Evelyn, who edited this book: your hard work, criticism and encouragements always bring me to higher levels than what I could ever achieve alone. Thank you!

Resources

Writing prompts

Here are a few good websites for writing prompts. In addition to them, there are many free apps you can download for your smart phone to send you a daily writing prompt.

http://www.writersdigest.com/prompts
http://writingprompts.tumblr.com/
http://awesomewritingprompts.tumblr.com/
http://www.reddit.com/r/WritingPrompts/
http://www.theteacherscorner.net/daily-writing-prompts/
http://postsecret.com/ .

Online mind-mapping software

http://bubbl.us/

Relaxation techniques:

In addition to the site below, you can find many relaxation audio CDs for free at your local library.

http://www.mayoclinic.org/healthy-lifestyle/stress-management/in-depth/relaxation-technique/art-20045368

Ergonomics:

There are many resources to explore ergonomics. These focus more on office ergonomics, which you are more likely to need as a writer, but you can research other kinds of ergonomics. Don't forget that these are guidelines, and you should compare and see what works best for you.

http://ergo.human.cornell.edu/dea6510/dea6512k/ergo12tips.html
http://www.ccohs.ca/oshanswers/ergonomics/office/
http://www.safety.uwa.edu.au/health-wellbeing/physical/ergonomics/workstation

Character Questionnaire

I. General
What is his or her name? Do they have nicknames, or alternative identities?

What do they do for a living?

Where do they live? (Country, city, type of home (apartment? House? Cardboard box?) Do they have other living arrangements, elsewhere? Who do they live with?

To what economic and social class do they belong?

II. Physical description
Age? Gender (and gender identity?)

Are they tall? Short? Round? Skinny? Lean?

What is the color of their eyes? Hair? Do they dye their hair? What is their skin tone?

Do they have anything that stands out? A really large nose? Eyes that are weirdly close together? Ears that really stick out on either sides? A huge gap between their two front teeth? How do they feel about that?

Do they have tattoos? Scars? Piercings?

II.1: Style
What kind of clothes do they wear? Do they wash them often? How important is appearance to them?

What kind of shoes do they like? Do they have one pair that will eventually die, or could they conceivably wear a different pair every day of the year?

Do they have jewelry? A lot, or always the same pieces? Do they have other accessories? (pocket watch, purse, cell phone, hat, etc.) If so, is it a question of style, or because they are practical, or because they are attached sentimentally to these things?

Do they wear make-up? A lot, or a little? Every day, or on special occasions?

Do they bite their nails? Do they care if their outfits match? What about their socks?

Would they change their clothes depending on where they go, or do they wear the same thing, no matter what?

II.2: Health
Are they particularly gifted in one or more areas? Or particularly NOT gifted?

Right or left-handed? What does their voice sound like?

Are they generally in good shape? Could they run a marathon just like that? Do they take the stairs or the elevator?

Do they have any chronic illnesses? Disabilities? Allergies?

Do they smoke? Drink alcohol? How much? Do they consume drugs? Are they addicted to them? Have they tried to stop? Why?

Are they dependent on a medication for their continued good health?

III. Family, lovers and friends
In general, how do they treat people? How do they treat animals? Children? The elderly?

Who is the person that matters most to them, and why?

Who is the person they respect most, and why?

Who is the person they hate most, and why?

III.1: Lovers
Do they have one or more current lovers? If so, what is their relationship with them?

How many ex-lovers do they have? What is their current relationship with them? Do they get along? Why did they break up?

Do they have a love interest that differs from their current lover(s)? What is their relationship with them? Why are they not with them, instead of their current lover(s)?

III.2: Family
Who are/were their parents? What kind of relationship do they have with them?

Any brothers and sisters? What's their relationship like?

Children? What is the relationship like?

Any other members of the family who have played a significant role (cousins, uncles, aunts, grandparents, others)?

III.3: Others
Who are their friends? Where did they meet? Do they have a best friend? What's their relationship like?

Do they have a roommate? Do they get along?

What about their colleagues? People they go to school with? Bosses? Ex-bosses? Professors? What about their neighbors? Do they talk to them?

Do they have someone that they consider a mentor?

If they were to die, who would find their body? Who would call the police if they went missing? Who would be sad? Happy? Worried? Affected in some other way?

IV. Past
Date and place of birth.

Where did they grow up? Under what circumstances? What kind of child were they?

Where did they go to school? Did they like school? Did they do well? Did they get along with the other kids?

Who were their role-models?

What was their relationship with their family like?

What did they want to be when they grew up? Has it changed? What were their favorite activities as a child? Are they still the same?

Where, when, how and with whom did their first kiss happen? Their first sexual encounter? Their first love affair? Have they ever really been in love?

What do they consider being the most significant moment in their life? The most embarrassing? The scariest? What is their deepest regret? Their best accomplishment? What is the worst thing they've ever done?

What is their happiest memory? Their worst? Their very first?

Do they have a criminal record? Why?

V. Psychology and personality
V.1: General
What is their main motivation? Their main ambition? What do they see themselves doing in five years? What is their definition of success?

What do they want out of life, and what do they need? (they're not the same!!)

Are they pessimistic or optimistic? Are they spontaneous, or would they rather always know where they're going?

What is the thing that irritates them most? Are they introverted, or extraverted?

What is their best quality? Their worst flaw? What are they most afraid of? Do they have a lot of fears or anxieties? What makes them most happy? Sad? Angry?

What are their religious and political convictions? Their relationship with money?

Do they have prejudices? What offends them the most? What is, according to them, the worst thing that a human being could do? Would they be capable of killing? Why? What would they be willing to die for? What would they never be willing to do, no matter what?

How do they deal with stress? With crowds?

What is their attitude towards life? Towards death? Towards sex? Love? Marriage? Monogamy? Family? Children? Do they believe in love at first sight? In true love? What is their sexual orientation? What do they look for in a potential partner?

Are they honest with their thoughts and feelings, or more reserved or deceitful? Do they care what others think of them?

Do they have any particular mannerisms? Expressions? What is their skill level with language?

If they could choose, how would they die? What would they do on their last day of life?

Do they have any mental illnesses or disabilities?

V.2: Education and other abilities

What is their highest level of education? How many degrees do they have? What did they major in? Did they receive any professional skills training? Where did they receive their degrees, or training? Why did they choose to study that?

Do they have any other trainings in particular? (e.g. martial arts, first aid, candy-making, etc.)

Are they well-read? Illiterate? Somewhere in between?

How many languages do they speak?

What are their hobbies? Any other activities that are not related to work?

What are they best at? What did they get picked last to do all their life?

V.3: Favorites and most hated things? Write both!

Food – drink – activity – sport – alcohol – music – books – fine arts – animal – color – entertainment – season – holiday – weather – clothing – place – humor – personal possession – way to spend a Saturday night – place to shop – anything else you can think of!!

What three words would THEY use to describe themselves?

UNBLOCKED

What three words would the people that know them use to describe them?

If you could give them a piece of advice, what would it be?

About the Author

Caroline Fréchette is a sequential artist and author. She has published four novels, several short stories, both sequential and traditional, as well as two graphic novels. She was the editor and director for the French Canadian literary magazine *Histoires à boire debout,* and works in a library. She has been teaching creative writing since 2005. Whenever she's not writing, she's making pictures and games. For more information, you can visit her website at carolinefrechette.com.

A WORD FROM THE AUTHOR

I hope this book was everything you hoped, and that it helped you get past whatever was blocking you. I have been teaching for a long time, and writing about writing for many years and you can find a lot of free information about writing on my website. Also, if this book did not solve your problem, please, contact me at **http://carolinefrechette.com/** to let me know, and I may be able to address your specific problem in a blog post.

I also offer a lot of author services, including coaching; if you thought this book was helpful to you, it is possible you might want to look into these services. Because you purchased this book, I am offering a special 10% discount on everything you might want on my site: just mention the book when you contact me for a quote.

Finally, if you enjoyed this book, please take the time to leave a review where you purchased it.

www.ingramcontent.com/pod-product-compliance
Lightning Source LLC
Chambersburg PA
CBHW051347040426
42453CB00007B/446